RAPUNZEL IN SUBURBIA

RAPUNZEL IN SUBURBIA

DOROTHY HEWETT

PRISM

Published with the assistance of the Literature Board
of the Australian Council for the Arts

First printed and published in 1975

Published by *New Poetry* for the Poetry Society of Australia
Box N110 Grosvenor Street Post Office
Sydney, NSW, 2000 Australia

Cover Paining: "I Lock the Door Upon Myself" *Fernand Khnopff*

Printed by Tonecraft Pty. Ltd., 24b Stanley Street, Peakhurst 2210
and wholly set up by Service Lino Pty. Ltd., Bankstown

Designed by Robert Adamson

ISBN 0 85869 008 X

Four grey walls, and four grey towers,
Overlook a space of flowers,
And the silent isle embowers
   The Lady of Shalott.

    Tennyson.

Also by Dorothy Hewett:
Bobbin Up (a novel), 1959
Windmill Country (poems), 1968
The Chapel Perilous (a play), 1972
Sandgropers (edited Anthology), 1973

*This book is dedicated to
friends & lovers,
sons & daughters.*

*I would also like to thank the Commonwealth
Literary Fund for the Fellowship that makes
this book possible, and my husband, Merv Lilley,
for his unfailing/failing love and support.*

CONTENTS

CONTENTS

RAPUNZEL IN SUBURBIA

ACKNOWLEDGEMENTS

Some of the poems in this book first appeared in the following publications: *Overland, Westerly, Meanjin, Poetry Australia, New Poetry and Australian Poetry 1968, 1970, '71, '72.*

MEMOIRS OF A PROTESTANT GIRLHOOD

There she weaves by night and day
A magic web with colours gay.
She has heard a whisper say,
A curse is on her if she stay
  To look down to Camelot.
She knows not what the curse may be,
And so she weaveth steadily,
And little other care hath she,
    The Lady of Shalott.

Memoirs Of a Protestant Girlhood

I

I was brought up on Tennyson and Eliot.
What a double! On the yellow farm
floated like The Lady down a creek,
lying on my back the sun motes danced,
black cockatoos massed shrieking in the sky.
My little sister whinged,
my mother rang her bells,
I lived alone: the pages riffled
in the afternoons bound in morocco
temperatures soared, round tables cracked,
Grandma draped wet hessian round the house.
Queen of the May! I had a melancholy decline.

Later I walked dry grass,
arms full of water hyacinths, met your eyes,
between the pencil pines the Sisters paced
howling like altars, schoolgirls twined
their magpie beaks for summer pools,
the fat Headmistress read "The Wasteland"
right through in a tinny voice, her 3 chins
                             quivered;
blood on my legs I swooned on the cane lounge.

[16]

II

Under a belljar in the sitting room
one Gawk was playing "Girl with the Flaxen Hair."
We sat about nonchalantly draped, rugs, sofas,
manes, beaked nose, a knee, my guilty passion!
The paddocks heated, dimmed through smokey glass
The Lady floated, brushed her hair & wept,
flung out dead hyacinths in a pained surprise.
Your mother, in her green habit, cut the heads
off roses, recited "Sonnets from the Portuguese."
Above the river as we ran to swim,
the pisspot mouthed us from her broken pane.
I lay in the sleepout burning for your bed,
thought on my father playing Serenades,
my mother safe in baby sister's arms:
my tin canoe, sliding past Camelot ·
                              to the Thames bank.
sank full   fathoms   five.

III

Before the altar, see, I kneel, I smile,
dust rises from the cushions, the priest stutters,
the gramophone wheezes "I'll walk beside you,"
in red crepe-de-chene vowing eternal love,
thinking of you, my witness & my bridesmaid,
clad as a bank clerk in this holy place.
So thus & thus I cleanse my guilty passion
& drunk in bed (the bridegroom in long johns
sobs for his mother) have nightmare honeymoon.
Ill-fitting, khakied, he leaves for the front,
I fornicate on beaches, mime adulterous passions,
        curettes in the dark,
looking like Dietrich slumming,
drive with a roughneck, in a black beret;
his Silver Anniversary Buick braves the desert,
you catch a bus up through the stoney ridges,
scribbly gums, to visit, meet the bridegroom
        weeping,
holding the baby, full of recriminations.

Now here we sit, kitchened, confined,
sprinklers play Auld Lang Syne,
you hand me poems I wrote
in an autograph album 30 years ago;
how they burn under your hydrangeas.
Above the garden,
the Anglican cross leans from St. Mary's spire.

Easy . . .

> look your last
> on that pewter river flashing swords
> the gas fire prickling red on virgin knees,
> my mother's bumpkin shape between the sun,
> rolled up the blinds & hung the afternoon,
> my father, beautiful Anzac, wonky-hearted,
> hawked over the fire-escape,
> his globule of spit spun like a catherine wheel,
> my sister playing Brahms by the smokers' stand,
> the black cat twined & purred in the cassia tree . . .
>
> down to wormy death
> between a breath & a breath,
> easy when you're young . . .
> > > **easy.**

Death Of My Mad Mother

To die quietly,
        one finger on "Legend of the Nineties"
marking his place,
the long night's tide pulling him
                through dream to dark.
Not like her, struggling, one side gone,
eyes fixed with implacable blame
                demanding love.
"Die!" I sob, "Die!"
& that indomitable voice whispers
                "I'm still here."
So that's the end of it,
                the long-days' hatreds,
Honey-top in the chair gone
                grey with waiting.

Calling On Mother

Look! the moths are out again,
eating giant holes in eiderdowns,
silverfish & mother's mothballs
                    clanking in the wardrobe.
NAPTHALENE   O HOW I LOVE YOU
                    NAPTHALENE!

Mother, Mother,
a man is exposing himself
under the black horsehair sofa.

Mother, Mother,
the sun's going down,
there's a madman rattling the long French doors
in the bedroom.
The wind shakes   &   shakes,
the knob comes off in my hand.

Mother, Mother,
the bloodstained rags are soaking in the pail.
MAKE THE TEA MOP UP THE BLOODSTAINS
            WRITE 100 TIMES
"I must not tell lies against my mother."

Mother, gigantic in her swami slips,
rubs & rubs at her Aladdin lamp
but never dips the wick.
Dress preservers sewn into armpits,
rubber corsets breathing holes of fat,
false teeth that never fitted
                    gnaw in cupboards.
PARAPHERNALIA   O HOW I LOVE YOU
                    PARAPHERNALIA!

Behind the wash-house masturbate & weep

        TWO & TWO MAKE FOUR
        FOUR & FOUR MAKE NINE!

Chafed raw I ran & learnt to answer "Mrs."
God save me & forget you not . . .

I've Made My Bed, I'll Lie On It

With legs apart I lie on mother's bed,
disturbing dust that shrouds the mighty dead.
You stake me out; as I begin to moan
her hairbrush beats us like a metronome.
She snicks her death's head over us with pins,
we fall apart, the bed's small hell begins.
An epitaph to end the fearful ride,
my heart, recalcitrant, leaps from my side:
seizing a chance I plagarize a line,
"With thee contending I forget all time;"
staking a bid for permanence I weep,
you give me up, roll over, fall asleep.

My tongue's a broken clapper in a bell,
with book and candle I roll down to Hell,
and circling back upon my mother's bed,
gift-wrapped receive the Kingdom of the Dead.

This Version Of Love

I have seen her, wonderful!
A waterfall of hair, body like glass,
Wading through the goldfish pools in winter,
Her white shark-skin dress dark-wet above her thighs,
The very shape and effigy of love:
Or turbanned, earringed, lying on the lawn
Among the clover burrs, her bangles clacking,
                            reading Ern Malley.
Oh! her nipples under her black lace bras
And flimsy blouses, her gold hair pins
Strewn in the car upholstery.

In the bar of the O.B.H. the creme de menthe
Slopped in the green squid bottles on the shelf,
The rain beat in great waves, running down
                            the plate glass windows.
On V.E. day a Yank gob somersaulted through
A jagged icy cut-out in the air,
Crusted with drops of blood.
"Shall I marry?
            Who shall I marry?
            Shall I die now
Swallowing lysol one glittering afternoon
Before my breasts fall and my womb tilts?"
Salt and water, the stomach pump
Coils like an evil creeper, wraps her round,
Choking and arching in the public ward.
In the queues outside the abortionist's
The white statues of cupids tumble at her feet.

The police-woman stands righteous beside her bed.
"Next time you try it you won't get away with it."
Obliterate me, save me, I go down
Hanging by my hair into the great avenues
                            of dust and leaves."

Fugitive as morning light she moves
In a thin rain out and across the river
                            leaving no footprints.

AH! THOSE DEAD LADIES

But in her web she still delights
To weave the mirror's magic sights,
For often thro' the silent nights
A funeral, with plumes and lights,
        And music, went to Camelot:
Or when the moon was overhead,
Came two young lovers lately wed;
'I am half sick of shadows,' said
        The Lady of Shalott.

Ah! Those Dead Ladies

"Come through the glass Sally,
        come through the glass,
come where the dead blue ladies pass,
come through the glass Sally,
        come through the glass."

("The Chapel Perilous")

I

That house has gone
        idealised now
        like other houses.
Thumb-prints washed from curtains,
boys weep in lavatories,
water breaks on mattresses,
the garden's wild, the neighbours all complaining.
Girls marry in wet white satin
                on the lawns,
the chlorinated pools are blue with children;
                these fiery circles
                woven by wistaria.

Last night, a gale:
I thought we'd go
under the Tasman Sea.
Ceilings fell on bedsteads,
        ambulances howled,
the two old sisters whinged
        all night in the attic.
The hare rose in Centennial Park
        and danced till dawn,
Henry Parkes, Diana and Hercules
sailed under the Moreton Bays
where the rape packs wait,
        to drown their girls
in the duckponds of memory . . .

This morning they were out,
            tending the maidenhair,
arm in arm, unshakeable as mist,
scraping the aphis off the roses.
Coming suddenly into a room,
            with chrysanthemums,
I catch them between the glass
            and open shutters.
Music brings them,
            pitifully out of tune
            by the open piano.
"They were sweet old things
                but mad.
Two sisters, a brother, parted
            how they cried!
But it ended happily,
            all loonies together
            in Ryde. It was nice for them."

Fern baskets swing in the rain,
ivy trails on trellises,
hands touch locks smudge glass
breathes catch fingers close
together   ah!   those dead ladies.

II

"She let all the rooms,
locked the mad one up in the shed
            to catch pneumonia.
They carried her out, feet first,
through the streaming ivy.
The old horse coughed and ran,
the imbecile drove the hearse,
            his coat tails flapping.
The landlady sat bolt upright,
            her hatpin gleamed,"
says truthful Jack
            under his caustic soda.

[27]

"Years later she came to the gate,
          hand on the latch,
          her 4 wits strayed.
'I'm going home,' she said.
They sent the green cart,
the old brother crowed clapped
          wept in the windows.
'You're welcome,' he said,
so she climbed in   smiling,"
          says caustic Jack
          with his tinful
                    of truthful soda.

"Velia, ah! Velia,
          the witch of the wood,"
          plays the pianola
          under the pimpling rain.

By her iron bedstead
the carpets worn white in a ring,
the hare dances,
the pervert exposes himself
                    in diminishing
                              circles . . .

"Would I not die for you
                    dear if I could,"
          plays the pianola
                    behind the pearling pane.

In Moncur Street

It's twenty years ago and more
since first I came to Moncur Street,
and lived with Aime and Alf among
the boarders on the second floor.

The stew was burnt, the budgie sang,
as Aime walked home the church-bells rang,
she banged the pots, ring-ding-a-ding,
she'd lost at Housie in the Spring.

But Sammy Smiles (that lovely man),
still visits her on Saturday,
Beat runs a book, and little Fay
whines in the stairwell every day
                    in Moncur Street
                    in Moncur Street.

Alf rose before the morning light,
and took a chopper in his hand;
he chopped and chopped in Oxford Street.
"Alf runs around without his head,
he's like a chook," said Aime
                    and sighed
for Sammy Smiles (that lovely man),

and Sunny Corner where she played
at "Ladies" in the willow's shade.
At sunset by the empty shops
they swapped their dusty acid drops:
who lounges in the crystal air,
but Sammy Smiles, with marcelled hair!

I woke up in the darkest night,
knew all the world had caught alight.
The surf was pounding in the weather,
and Moncur Street was mine forever.
The little bat upon the stair
came out and flapped: it wasn't there,

the snapshot album turned and turned,
the stew caught fire, the budgie burned,
the pensioners at drafts and dreams,
picked bugs between their trouser seams.

And Sammy Smiles (that lovely man!)
and Aime and Alf and little Fay,
and Beat and Bert and betting slips,
the man I loved, the child I bore,
have all gone under Bondi's hills,
and will return here nevermore,
                    in Moncur Street
                    in Moncur Street.

Alf starts up his steady snore,
"Them Bondi sandhill's paved with gold,
I could've bought them for a song."
The home brew bursts behind the door.
Aime lies upon her back and sighs:
"In Sunny Corner by the store
Sam kissed me once when I turned four."

Dreams are deep and love is long:
she turns upon her other side.

Drowned Child

Seven days rolled in the Autumn tide,
the child swung home and rose
in Shoalhaven Bay.

Crabs at her lips,
the blue flesh barnacled
she metamorphosed on the empty beach,
come back from there with trailing arm
a fin a down of hair cast in a pool.

Seven days a wonder, sailors wept
and knelt to see her pass, the currents
turned her face towards home.
What home,
what shore can take her now,
not fish or child but beast
magicked from ruin in the pearly deep.

Anemones open,
from her gaping sides
the sea grapes cluster,
none dare to touch,
        she floats and she divides.

Forsaken Mermaid

The maimed mermaid on Bondi cliff,
arms lopped, struck to her knees,
yearns towards her sister
              gone to the pounding seas.

She swims deep water
              under circling gulls,
stone arms round drowned sailors,
              cold kiss on their skulls.

Her blank eyes stare at the rim,
where the skies meet the seas,
she rocks, cradles & hums,
              her stone arms squeeze.

With her we cannot identify,
she is the self gone free,
the wild girl in the heart
              tied to no man,
no child, but haunts the sea.

Would we change places with her,
out there where the tide turns,
sufficient and sunless as self,
              who cannot suffer or burn?

Maimed mermaid left on the cliff,
trembling in stone,
remind us of our dear human predicament,
              imprisoned, alone.

The Witnesses

This is the wide country
I lived in when I was young,
The great clouds over it,
The hawk in the high sky hung. . . .

Hung upside down like a metal bird,
Fixes time in his fatal eye.
The mice run circles, the plovers cry,
Till I hardly know in that hurtling sky
Which of the three wild things am I . . .
Murderer, victim, recorded cry.

The hawk spins round like a weather vane.

The seed spills bitter, the hawk turns slow.
Under the rainbow arch will lie
The girl with the haystack hair awry,
Her legs outflung and her brief blood dry,
While the bumpkin boys go whistling by
with gravel rashed knees and weeping eye. . . .

And the hawk in the high sky hung.

House That Jack Built

Rib-cage open to the sun,
it comes true to itself,
dry stalks and winter reeds.

Walls spin with water shadow,
birds impress themselves on glass.

My mad green house
heavy with windy chimneys,
when I wake at dawn
in a brass bedstead
tilted into the grass,
hear the kingfishers
picking in the clearing,
I'm afraid we've lost
some old dark hidden self.
Hornets, spiders, sepia photographs,
oil lamps with blown glass-fluted shades,
crippled men rubbing Sloan's liniment,
thickened the rooms with the mystery of being.

The old woman lit the grate,
pushed the boat from the reeds,
fished the river, one pelican
floating on either side.

'We sailed on the kitchen table,
the mud was 3-feet up,
tea-roses ruined on the carpet.
It's out on the verandah
    if you want to *look* at the river.'

Now that we've let in the swallows,
we've driven out the ghosts,
mad as hatters, down on their knees,
touching the tea-roses up
        with water-colours.

Sun seals their cataracts,
we live, riddled with light,
under our dubious roof-tree.

Turn around,
who is the girl in the mirror
with the white heron blinking on her shoulder?

The Single Cry

If we lived here all summer
with the river under our windows
and the swallows from Hang Chow
looping across the water . . .
would we write poems, would novels
stream from our pens, would the puppets
from our plays jerk on the front lawn
under the wattle pods, cracking and splitting open . . .

Or, sometimes, at first light,
would we climb from our iron bedstead
in dressing gowns, and sit at the windows
feeling the river, rising and dark,
at the end of the garden;
hear the fuchsias open in the dew
under the leaking tankstand,
the leaves move on the walls,
the clock without hands
tick under the blue convolvulous . . .

Our arms wrapped round each other,
trembling at the open windows like ancient shadows,
the batteries run down,
the typewriters silent,
would we go to our unremembered graves
in the Pinjarra churchyard,
under the mullioned windows
            without a single cry . . .

Let Candid Speech At Last . . .

In old age I will learn to use my tongue
And all this babble turn to speech at last.

Until then how can I endure a slack mouth?

I brayed incessantly when I was young.
For eight dumb years words lay beyond my reach

The iron clapper swollen up in my mouth.

Hard, fine and passionate, can language glow
Like ice and fire, both luminous and cool

A benediction falling from the mouth?

And yet there seems no guarantee to know
If, in old age, I still can play the fool

Suck a dry socket in an aching mouth.

And all this endless struggle, all the stones
Of words that trip and weigh upon my tongue

May serve me nothing but an old wet mouth.

Perhaps that braying voice from the bones,
The eight dumb years, the wisdom dry and wrung

Will bounce like polished pebbles in my mouth.

What a rag harvest will I pick over then,
The crazy mirror and the splintered eye

Will all reflect an old woman's wailing mouth.

Well, some grow cataracts and some old men
Rage in a tarnished glass until they die.

Let candid speech at last fall from my gaping mouth.

Sanctuary

"Who's the old doll reading her poetry under the light?"
*   *   *

The winter's coming on,
the air swarms with leaves.
Driven in,
they gather in our house.
Outside the massacre begins.
The unsheathed razor,
footprints marked in blood,
pills spilt from a pack:
I have known the terror.
I gather them in
to the light's ambience;
it bathes a faint small round.

The shelter falls apart,
the light wavers in water,
a round skull on a pole
I turn and turn,
a weathercock, a totem out of time
who cannot catch the moment.
I have visited the crematorium three times.

"She rose unsteadily from the night,
Took two of orange and one of white."

Old women wet their beds, cry softly,
rummage in each other's lockers, scavenge for life,
but the young lie like stone,
shrouded to the chin in a white sheet,
tubes draining the sleeping pills from every aperture.

She sits on a balcony in a private nursing home
in a white dress, skinny as a bone,
her head on a stalk nods from side to side,
a green creeper engulfs her from the world outside,
her eyes stare, she is still, listening, queer,
remembering the young husband who gassed himself last year

[38]

in the park, before the commuters came;
fixed the exhaust, wound up the windows, insane
people kill themselves; she locked the doors
and ate and ate, had food delivered from stores
in bulk, until they found her at last
and propped her on a balcony, a girl with a past
and no future, sitting up here alone
in a see-through dress in a private nursing home.

"She looks like Whistler's Mother!"

They grappled him out of the river: it was on T.V.
His parents watched, gripping the edge of their chairs
his hair turned white, his skin gone soggy: "It can't be him,"
they said. "He used to run along the foreshore in jockey shorts,
shining and scrubbed like . . . Colgates."
They'd been searching for him in the sandhills for days before,
falling over the homosexuals with their togs pulled down.
Someone had seen him running alone in the dunes.
It was cold that weekend, he kept his head well down,
and went on running when they called.
Somebody thought they heard him moving in the hills,
crying for sanctuary amongst the thorn and rocks.
The parson found him and led him into the nave.
Under the stained glass window he laid him down,
on his black chin the lozenges played, scarlet and blue.
While the parson phoned in the vestry he slipped away.
They called and called and got out the dogs,
but all the time he was lying dead in his boat-bay
with three anchor chains wrapped round his body, like Christ
hauled out of the river, glittering wet in the arc lamps,
                                        a spearing marlin!
and somebody else was crashing about through the hills,
unwashed, sleepless, a revolver cool on his ribcage.

This nervous hollow city is built on sand,
looped with wires, circled with shaven trees.
The bleeding pidgeons tumble outside the windows,
the children wring their necks.
The exchange is jammed with outward calls,
the T.V. screen, jagged with light,
crackles and goes out.

The boy on drugs, his bandages slipping,
argues and pleads all day with the parking meters.
The filthy children of Christ lie on mattresses in the sun,
the pavement scrawled with graffiti, in excrement and blood.

Bare-footed children driven out over the plain,
thorny the mallee and spinifex, thumbing a ride interstate,
do not call me again and reverse the charges.
Winter is coming on.
I have dialled three times.
The whole city is engaged in a kind of slaughter.

I am only an old doll reading her poems in the lamplight,
waiting for a fourth cremation.

O! BABY, BABY,
IT'S A WILD WORLD

She left the web, she left the loom,
She made three paces through the room,
She saw the water-lily bloom,
She saw the helmet and the plume,
      She look'd down to Camelot.
Out flew the web and floated wide;
The mirror crack'd from side to side;
"The curse is come upon me!" cried

    The Lady of Shalott.

Living Dangerously

O to live dangerously again,
meeting clandestinely in Moore Park
the underground funds tucked up between our bras,
the baby's pram stuffed with illegal lit.
We hung head down for slogans on The Bridge,
the flatbed in the shed ran ink at midnight.

Parked in the driveway, elaborately smoking,
the telltale cars, the cameras, shorthand writers.
Plans for TAKING OVER. .3YRS.THE REVOLUTION.
The counter revs. out gunning for the cadres.
ESCAPE along the sea shelf, wading through
        warm waters soft with blood.
WOW! WHAT A STORY! . . . guerrilla fighters
wear cardigans and watch it on The Box,
lapsed Party cards, and Labour's in again.
Retired, Comrade X fishes Nambucca Heads,
& Mrs. Petrov, shorthand typist,
                hiding from reporters
                brings home the weekly bacon.

But   O   O   O   to live
            so dangerously again,
their stamina trousers pulling at the crutch.

Alice In A German Garden

Do you remember the garden in the watery sunlight . . .
Delphiniums, striped canvas swings rocking the bald-headed
    writers?
We dodged the shadows of ravens swooping down out of the
    boughs,
                 Searching for eyes and hearts.
The young spies struggled manfully in the flower borders,
Clutching and cocking giant Salvador Dali ears
That pulled their bodies sideways like fleshy tape-recorders
Hung upside down in the shrubbery behind our heads.

We are caught here, embedded in glass under the plastic flowers
At the foot of Heine's statue; our American voices echo
Across the borders, harsh with chain smoking and endless
    coughing
In misty gardens: the thirties created us, McCarthy made us
    immortal,
The Cold War embalmed us; we creak in the wicker chairs
Under the linden trees in a strange climate: the high falsetto
Of the huge Negro tenor, carolling his thin German lieder
Out in the provinces, caught soliciting pretty boys
Along the Unter den Linden . . . it was all hushed up
For his faded little Eva, refugees out of a Faulkner mythology
    tale:
The drawling Southern heat, the white dust, the plaster pillars
At the end of the long oleander avenue, the ricketty frame house
From a jerky movie, all lost, lost now, the black boy screaming
In the empty road, clutching his bloody genitals.
The exiles' voices float like a mockery in a second-rate light opera
Of peeling gilt and miniature velvet boxes . . . The Duchess is
    here,
The Dormouse diving his head in the priceless Sèvres teapot,
The punchbowl from Macey's shatters in rainbows on the grass,
Home movies: the Hollywood Ten unwrap their celluloid
    bandages,
The porch flickers with light and blood; the Red Queen
Douses her screams in the pan of the new American toilet.
"Alice, Alice will you come back next year
For the International Meeting of the Veterans of the Spanish Civil
    War?"

[43]

The motor boat rocks—its engine cut—at the foot of the garden
Reflected twice in the water; petrol is rationed; it will never
Take us down the gleaming front of the river to Günter Grass.
The industrialists have three chins, their napkins, snowy-white,
Foam on their waistcoats; crackling green-backed dollars
They spoon pink ice cream behind the plate-glass windows.
The Nazis are howling into their microphones in Bavaria.
The glass doors of the Hotel Berolina swing open automatically
At a footfall; the heated dome of light will sweat and swarm
With faces and the swimming bite of cognac on the tongue.
The Alsatians pace endlessly up and down the borders,
The Vopos click their rifles at Checkpoint Charlie.
Why do we all keep on meeting the same characters
Like a morality play; the taxi driver who snarls
"This country is shit", the young West German who married
The East German girl, and can't go home to mother,
The silent waiter who spits his contempt on the pavement?

"Did your books get through last month,
Or did you again receive only the dust jackets?
I have complained to the Ministry of Culture."

"My novel has been pulped, my heart beat is getting fainter,
What was the date on my last letter?" . . .
Oh! Alice, Alice, remember the beleaguered garden,
Remember the raven waiting in the linden tree.

You Gave Me Hyacinths First a Year Ago

The world's a stranger's room, we meet to part,
I stand, transfixed, an arrow through my heart.

My ageing Cupid, careful of his aim,
plucks out the shaft, and causes twice the pain.
My awkward arms are full of brandy, sin,
helpless I watch our promenade begin.

Hands touch, eyes falter, tremble, fix and cling,
the heart leaps up, the blood beneath the skin
tingles like frost, then all disguise is shed,
until he husks me naked in my bed.

My hyacinths are nettles, the cold breath
of the Toad Prince is in my ear like death.
"What will become of us?" "We'll live to die,"
and in that restless void, disfigured, lie
forever, and forever answer, "No."
Contending on heaven's plain we'll weep and go.

So without choice, and convinced of doom,
I go to meet you in the stranger's room.

Underneath The Arches

I wear black now,
the witch's clothes.
Portents, omens, stab me in the dark.
Old age is either pastels, twin-sets, pearls of
            gentle wisdom, or else a robe of power.

A difficult sleight of hand—
to remain vulnerable to experience,
yet closed in the black cloak of flesh.

To stand open in a wooden O
            is always risky,
but a cyclorama of small orbs, a moon,
a skyrocket or two, is never vulgar,
and cosmic imagery is right in fashion.

The impudent terror of the lady sawed in half,
for that one needs the magic nudity—
34   24   34.

If you didn't drop dead in the Tiv,
            A Marcus *Girl*,
suffocated in a tight skin of gilded flesh,
mourned by Lennie Lower, Mo and Cine-
sound,
don't haunt the massage parlours:
G-strings don't snap on hairy terrors.

But power is something else:
to write a poem
Dame Edith Sitwell
bade the London jackhammers cease,
and Nellie Melba (with insomnia)
stopped the Town Hall clock in Bendigo.

Dissolving in a spotlight
          keep your cool
with a pack of tarot cards
And jiggery-pokery behind a screen.
*Gentlemen may remove any garment consistent with
          decency.*
Ladies may remove any garment consistent with charm.

Hand Waving

In Melbourne rain,
in Canberra cold,
you were everywhere,
ghost in the mind,
tranquillized, one hand waving
   above the sheets.

Oranges from a tin,
Angela Davis,
    fantasies of Rome.
We shared the Grt. October Revolution,
phone calls, crow calls:
sealed in my motel room
the air conditioner hums
late night cowboy movies,
seven stories down
   a body splats
scattering the wrought iron chairs.

A haunted city,
granite, bluestone,
Collins St canyons of rock.
I danced on the St Kilda tramlines,
"HENRY BOLTE IS THE POOR MAN'S FRIEND!"

Planes take off,
every airport plays
   enchanted evenings.
"HAWKS FACE CRISIS AT WINDY HILL!"
"What a game to come back on!"
A heartbeat stops . . .
The Big Sleep,
crow call, phone call,
   valium, brandy,

and a hand waving
   wav - ing.

This Time

I

The rain falls, the wind
blows in the canyons of the University.
Drinking with the Professor of English
behind the plate-glass windows
the last crocus is whipped to death.

Heidelberg paraplegics; the boy dies in the iron lung,
his 21 kindly candles winking in the last light on the balcony;
the ice-caked windscreen fogs, the Flame of Remembrance
burns like hell-fire in the wintry air by the Psychiatric Clinic;
the light, like a faulty film, slips from my detached retina in the
   Eye Hospital.

Your house is a mausoleum, the springing lids
of Victorian jewel boxes click in the stillness,
the stuffed monkey swings in the cupboard behind your eyes.
The white terrace creaks in the wind;
I lie like a seed curled in the body of the house,
The footsteps troop up the stairs
and circle my bed to judge me.
I wrestle on the floor, in a harsh light,
               with an old familiar angel,
our mutual friends give me a cheek to kiss.
Outside in the dark the magpies whistle;
at the foot of the stairs in the empty hall each evening
the kitten places my black fur glove like a clue.

[49]

It will soon be over.
I wrap myself in a black cloak
to hide with the English Department in the cafeteria,
but when you come towards me
my body husks and I cling to your hands.

I am too tired,
I will travel centuries of escalators to Richmond,
and think of you all night in Paddy's Market
                amongst the refugees from Katmandu.
I sit with the Catholic poets;
(a relic of some dim Pre-Raphaelite girl)
they understand the nature of suffering,
and my times with you are all like
                Stations of the Cross.
A night of Merka's dolls:
I discover them, imprisoned in paperweights,
moon faces float darkbeaked above the tide,
their fishtails flick with grief.
I will fly to Sydney, weeping like a dolphin.

III

In the garden, in the morning,
I was like Eve,
I was like sin in red velvet,
I walked barefoot
till my hem was wet, the globes spun
on the lemon trees your body's weight,
the sun came up, my children slept.
With my hands full of winter flowers
I enter my own house
and open the Art Exhibition.
As we drive home across the winter city,
the dark comes down with birds.
My words lash out like hail,
hunched over the wheel you don't protect yourself.
Lucky Untouchable! you are always guilty.
The airport swarms, some terminal in hell.
We swap quotations;
"And thus contending on the plains of Heaven;"
hands part, I'm on firm ground;
"With thee conversing I forget all time."
Take me to Beechworth, cover me with kisses.
Where my great-neverending-grandmother served Ned Kelly,
I could be one of your green ladies.
You will never go in search of the woman you love,
casting her sacred pots in some London suburb.
I watch you walk away, incestuous twin,
miracle and monster, my other self.
A black swan floats, broken-necked in the Airport pool,
stoned by innocence.

Planes overhead:
I take to the freeway, driving fast and cold,
looking for a fix.
In the empty house the imprint of your head
on a leather chair; I strip the bed
and leaving, look back once.
Shut in my study I teach them "Paradise Lost."

[51]

IV

I've made it once again,
gone past the pitch of grief,
each time it's easier and nonchalant.
Slip into it Old Friend; a fatal treaty.
I stretch my limbs, knowing the stages
of withdrawal, irony contributes,
(but not much) it's giving yourself to pain,
no twilight sleep, cold turkey!
It helps to be a woman, not in God's image.
I weep in terminals and public libraries.

It's over now,
the waking up to pain,
the compensatory eating's almost stopped.
On a diet I'm even interested in other men.
My calendar measures months.
My capacity for faithfulness was always limited.
Yet there's a dreariness, not visionary at all,
old flicks, old times,
the sepia snapshots in my family album:
Watergate breaks
its stoney teeth and bridge of sighs
flying Old Glory, the wiretappers' lament.
Flesh fails,
my bones are stiff, yet winter passes,
spring builds its hopes.
I find the same face in the bathroom mirror.
Hard to sink back again to middle-age.

Now that the pain has gone
I'm lost without it,
no rhythm to my days, no sense of purpose;
brute force, a wheel to break on
balanced time, but that's all lost.
I turn your letters in a drawer,
and think of words I wrote,
know the old itch for permanence
made these sly icons of ephemera.

[52]

But here's the proof we lived
to write each other from our distant cities,
suffered alone in motel rooms,
put out a hand, smiled, sat up naked,
shared each other's bodies . . .
phoney libertines and beautiful fucks!

Somewhere in a far city the night comes down,
                        (two hours early)
sound waves crackle, you die in bed
of a broken heart, your hand reaching
                        for the telephone
before the blackness cuts the last receiver;
I would have answered one long distance call.
You lie with the Sisters of Mercy
under the dangling man,
your ribcage cracked,
your side open to their hands.
"Jesus! but that was close!"
"We prefer, my son, to call it the will of God."
(We two non-believers, atheists to the end.)

I walk in the garden in the last light
and hear a bird call, but no soul sings out.
Your books are on my shelf, on the dust jackets
I trace your beardless face,

                younger . . . more vulnerable . . .
The engaged signal beeps mournfully through the house.

Politician

The Prince begets the King,
inherits the hollow crown,
the kingdom of smiles.

There by the librium pills,
        the brandy bottle,
pulling his cardigan round him
        from the cold,
The peacemaker lives his life
        of myth and ritual.

Behind his eyes,
the young Prince sits subdued,
the long-thighed girls
        he leapt upon in bed
with the hi-fi roaring,
are married, pregnant, penned,
        by other men,
the old cock lies limp
        between his legs.

In an ocean of voices
        he moves
— two resolutions.
His tongue forks phrases up
like shells, like milky pearls.

A wild voice cries . . .
"The Albatross is dead!"

Moon-Man

Stranded on the moon,
a librium dreamer in a lunar landscape,
the tabloids were full of your blurred, blown-up face,
the neat curled head, the secret animal eyes,
immolated forever in the Sea of Tranquillity.

I keep getting messages from outer space,
"Meet me at Cape Canaveral, Houston, Tullamarine."
A telegram came through at dawn to the Dead Heart Tracking
    Station.
I wait on winter mornings in hangars
dwarfed by grounded crates like giant moths
    furred with frost.

Moon-pictures — you dance clumsily on the screen,
phosphorescent, domed, dehumanized,
    floating above the dust,
your robot voice hollow as bells.

The crowds queue for the late edition,
scan headlines avidly, their necks permanently awry,
looking for a sign, a scapegoat, a priest, a king:
the circulation is rising.

They say you have been knighted in your absence,
but those who swear they know you best,
assert you are still too radical to accept the honour.

They have sent several missions,
but at lift-off three astronauts fried,
    strapped in their webbing.
Plane-spotters on penthouse roofs
have sighted more UFOs.

Sometimes I go out at night
    to stare at the galaxies.
Is that your shadow, weightless,
    magnified in light,
man's flesh enclosed in armour,
suffering eyes in perspex looking down,
sacred and murderous from your sanctuary?

Blue Movie

In black chiffon
I flee from the white mansion,
my contemporaries
(the death's head moths)
sit judging in the ballroom,
an old child I teeter past,
tall lesbians in bi-focals
            catch my hands,
the piano, soaked in claret,
starts up the Golden Oldies,
the white-haired guru passes
7 ft. tall bowing in the garden.
"O   look!   There's . . . X . . ."
the pouffes are full of chloroform,
my beautiful daughters sit,
iron maidens under their chandeliers.

I search for you
            above the geriatrics,
but you are taking snuff
            by the lilli pilli,
its red fruit stains
            your leather jacket.
The fat man follows me,
wire burns my palms,
I cling to the cyclone fence

CONFESS   CONFESS

"One night I'm afraid
            I'll come for you
a white-haired girl
lugging my nylon nightgown
            like chain armour."

Conversations

After all what's there to talk about,
a few fucks!
Thinking back on all our "conversations"
I can hear my cracked disc playing,
can't distinguish your replies.
Do I need a new needle or a replay?
Am I asking much?
Need to be noticed once every couple of yrs.
(who am I kidding) but when I spill my guts
even I want a feed back.

I can see myself
                100 yrs. old,
a wrinkled croc, meeting you in bars
                on sad weekends
                in violet light,
laying my head on your shoulder,
                endlessly arguing,
                me with my trident,
            you with your mended net.
"Haven't you had enough theatre yet?"
Will we play the play about how God
                came to Mahagonny?
I was brought here in a cab,
the driver my ex-defacto gone insane;
in the foyer, above his windcheater,
an ex-lover's blazing cheekbone
                stares me blind
Being dignified at the Opera
we escape onto the balcony,
in our arrowed suits we lean
                towards Pinchgut,
            some more simple prison.

Waiting to eat to Gershwin's
                "Summertime"
we posture like glass animals
seeing right through each other.

"You know me very well.
Think of all those who loved
                & suffered over you."
Who are they? I don't remember.

Both of us wearing well,
glorious victors; look,
  we drive towards power, cunning defeat,
  & self delusion, loving our heads,
  accepting & defeated, wearily knowing
  all, so take my hand, kiss me
  goodbye, your sister Jesus!
    I leave myself alone on the curb
    hailing my midnight cab to motel
    morning plane taking you south
    again, never mind — if I lose
    I write a poem about loss
                — & win.

Professor Quixote

He doesn't call anybody in now,
threatened behind the desk,
torturing his paper clips;
the long corridors, fitted with eyes,
mirror the piddling present,
the past goes by peddling his bicycle
                    in the clean air;
Cambridge and the Antipodes, another country.
new broom sweep clean, sweep clean.

The Professor who steps on knives,
his bloody footprints mark his morning walk.
My father surrogate, my father figure,
dwindling on the horizon,
whistles his black dog up against the endless light.

Retiring next year to his garden tower,
he does not tilt at windmills,
but sits in the whirling vanes,
above the darkening suburbs,
his retractable ladder always at the ready.

Miss Hewett's Shenanigans

They call, "The Prince has come,"
& I swan down in astrakan & fur,
the lemon curtains blown against the light,
the scent of lilac on the balconies.
In the entrance hall
the Prince is standing
                staring at my thighs.
He mounts, how cold the marble
underneath my buttocks.
As he rides he calls me
                "whore" & "princess".
A platinum crooner, old as Alice Faye,
belts out bad ragtime in the empty ballroom.
The Prince, buttoning his fly,
is doing push-ups & demanding saunas.
Two giant Ghanians smile & kiss my hand.

Snow piles like roses
                up against the panes,
the waiter brings "Ogonyok",
SINYAVSKY'S FLED & SOLZHENITSYN'S EXILED.
The lights all fail,
the electrician's pinching bulbs
from the chandeliers, shoving them
                down his shirtfront.
Outside in the dark at Lenin's tomb
they endlessly queue for weeping
                at the waxworks.
The Prince is in the Conference Hall,
listening through headphones
to a speech in seven languages.
Handsome Yugoslav colonels
discreetly try my doorknobs.
Exhausted, we sleep among carved bears
with ashtrays in their paws,
he refuses, once again, to consummate
                our marriage.

Next day we catch the Trans-Siberian
to Peking; from the observation car
we watch two wolves pacing out the train,
the Prince throws pennies to Manchurian children.
On the Great Wall he lets the wind blow
through my hair, in the Forbidden City
we listen to the clockwork nightingale.

By Aeroflot we fly in to Berlin,
the Prince will not declare his Camels
                    at Checkpoint Charlie,
(An international incident is narrowly averted.)
In the country house of Hitler's wormy mistress
we row on a lake circled with tubor roses.
The Prince, a playboy in a boater hat,
is picking the plastic flowers
                    off Heine's statue;
denouncing Nazis he pisses in the Weimar
                              fountain,
rides with a chignoned spy
                    down Karl Marx Allee.
Tiring of this,
          we climb across The Wall,
the Vopos bow, goosestep & fire a round,
the bullets spurt,
we show our elegant heels.
In West Berlin the Prince
calls for his breakfast, on TV
Brehznev has cancer, enters the Mayo clinic.

The Prince leafs through his autographs,
Picasso, Ghandi, Garbo, Pasternak,
calls Nabokov long distance, mounts me,
yawns, the Brandenburg Gate whirls
& explodes in the pale Autumn air.
Next morning he leaves,
                    taking all my roubles.

Suffering from migraine
I enter a Retreat
among the Alps I write him
endless letters.
The corridors are full of parasites,
consumptives haemorrhage in their sleety
                              deckchairs,
in the white nights I masturbate
                    my pillows.

    An aerogramme arrives,
    "The Prince is dead!"
I take up seances,
each night we couple,
circling the empty ballroom
              to "Moscow Nights."
Cockroaches rustle, my thrombosed knee
reeks of its vodka bandage,
the dust settles from the chandelier
          on his bald head . . .

RAPUNZEL IN SUBURBIA

And down the river's dim expanse—
Like some bold seer in a trance,
Seeing all his own mischance—
With a glassy countenance
Did she look to Camelot.
And at the closing of the day
She loosed the chain and down she lay;
The broad stream bore her far away

The Lady of Shalott.

Re-Union

"All other lovers being estranged or dead"—YEATS

Snared in the suburban drawing room
With my husband, my ex-husband and my ex-lover,
I sit alone Rapunzel, ah! Rapunzel let down your hair.
The eyes of my ex-husband's wife knife me miserably
For the past she can never share, except by proxy,
The eyes of my ex-lover's wife skin me alive.
(I rejoice at their private hatreds aired in public,
and shake at her revelations of domesticity.)
My husband's eyes regard me with irony.

My husband, my ex-husband and my ex-lover
Down their beers like men,
Talk politics, anthropology, conservation.
I sit naked at their feet,
The eyes of their women
Deliberately pluck out my backbone.

Under the sound of the reticulation system
Pouring against the glass, I hear his voice:
"Rapunzel how beautiful you are."
He claims me with his hand.
"No-one can hear us, no-one is listening."
My ex-husband bends to catch the murmured words,
Cuckolded once again.
A giant beast comes out of the garden
And settles at my side, the storm of water on the glass
Reflects my face, the sadness of menopause, the faltering body.
No-one can hear us, no-one is listening.

Protected by this room, he sits and smiles,
Aloud he says: "I've grown conservative,
A simple man, don't wish to be disturbed,
Content enough, my job, my wife, my children."
My husband's eyes regard me with irony.

We stalk the circle of ourselves, outside the women
Clamour to be let in: this is a private hell,
No place for ladies, only for wild sad girls
Who lie down under hedges with their legs apart
Crying for love, the privet in their hair.

The jungle of umbrella trees and tree fern
Presses the plate glass windows till they bulge and crack.
The bottle smashes on the carpet, the beer stain spreads,
Lapping at the feet of my ex-husband's wife.
She stands, islanded in grief, justice tipping her scales.

Under one roof you gather up my life
And rend it with your murderous paws.
My husband takes my arm, I exit in disgrace.
Rapunzel, ah! Rapunzel let down your hair.

Uninvited Guest

With her bare fat suffering feet,
With her head stuffed full of tranquillizers
                              and her ovaries removed,
My ex-husband's wife stands under the green potato plant
In her subterranean kitchen and hates me.

The potato plant grows and covers the walls and ceiling,
A climbing monstrous ganglia, green nerves, groping arms.
One day it will lovingly circle her throat and stop
                              her yammering heart.

Her delinquent boys piss over each other in bed,
                              crazy with laughing,
Her autistic girl's pale dopey eyes are blank with unconcern.
Her voice from an old table-model "His Master's Voice",
                              endlessly discusses her hysterectomy.

I watch him come in from his fish-ponds,
                              his hanging baskets of Babylon,
Myopic eyes fixed on some point in the middle distance.
Where are you while your wife sits strangling in a great green vine
                              in the kitchen,
Your sons are lying in sheets soaked with angry yellow urine,
Your daughter sits in a deep freeze, tranced out of hatred?

Once you danced "L'Aprés-Midi d'une Faune" in a green garden,
With an ancient parrot swearing away like a stable hand,
And the cumquats rosy, cloven on the trees,
The leaves made ferny patterns on our buttocks,
My breasts hung down like unpicked ripening cumquats,
My belly swelled with the child who died of cancer.

What poison did you carry in your genes?
All the bright children of your body turned to death,
The white flesh bruised as grapes under miniature tombstones.
I want to cry after you, "Rip off those cataracts",
But haven't the heart: we keep to our own towers
Locked in with our victims and our murderers.

Put on dark glasses and a blind man's head,
A blind man's listening uneasiness.
Sit still beside the tranced child on the bench,
The water lilies drowning at her feet.
The voice goes on and on through the kitchen gauze,
The locusts' drum, the river storms outside.

One day I will push open the wicket gate,
Go silently into the house and find you there
On the kitchen tiles, wrapped in each other's arms,
                    smiling serenely, choked black.
The boys make muffled water spouts under the bedclothes,
The potato plant rampages, curling and tendrilling
                    from tea-caddy to flour-bin to discarded
    flesh.

Weathercocks

Beneath the pinions of the swan
we sat and let our bodies turn
against a wintry sky and wan,
a convex touch, to melt, to burn.

Beneath the bird, north south and east,
or westering in a sudden squall,
two Ledas all that winter sat,
a twinned and female principle;
a cold beak nuzzling at our napes,
a talon probing at our will,
gripped fast beneath the darkening beast.
before the giddy fall   .   .   .   .

and still the swan whirls in my head
a paradox that cannot fly,
and staked upon our marriage bed,
two naked weathercocks we lie.

The Glass-House

In the crazed mirror of my eye
the world is flawed irrevocably,
I walk without the grace of sight,
who made my whole world visually.

What giant hand above my head
shattered the mirror of the sky,
and left me with a blinded face;
dependent on an inner eye
to recreate the universe,
to force into the face of light
a world so faceted and bright,

refracting light, reflecting love,
out of an eye so picked with pain,
that none can see it, none can build
such private glass-house in the brain.

But Lately I Stare At The World

Lately I stare at the world
as if I couldn't get enough of it,
chained to a spinning jenny.

You, over there, who carry on your shoulder
the other one, an image of what-self,
Jack-self, God's fool, more lunatic
than ever I imagined.

Each has his substance, each his mortal shadow,

each one walks innocent and nervous to his end.
Look behind! for God's sake look behind!
the mortal monkey leaps and clings.

I have a choice: close one eye and forget
or dare the two
but lately I stare at the world.

The Child

When first she came
we were afraid,
for moving she displaced the air,
as if some small and glittering shade
had from the fields of heaven strayed,
and circling in her hair,
upon the dull earth gravely played
her magic game.

But since she came
she passes by
so often that we've grown hard;
yet like a dust mote in the eye
her beauty troubles us, her cry
still shakes me: in the empty yard
I tremble that all things must die
and call and call her name.

Quick Now
(after re-reading Four Quartets)

It's a quick now, here now, always, moment:
the green wild garden under a cradling web,
the spring petals spilling in the rain,
the great white broken bodies of the statues
                              crumbling like flesh.
The new leaves furl, the fire burns
in time suspended, the ring dove swings
incessantly re-echoing that time.

I break the web, I hold the tight jaws back
                              to catch the moment.
Comfort me, the atheist chained in time,
                        the beast with memory.

Picasso's "Girl With Dove"

The girl in the blue dress with the dove in her arms
is standing forever in the curve of the hall.
Nobody notices her there:
she has merged into the curtain's shadow,
or the strange blue light that comes
from the pine tree outside the open window.
But I am always conscious of her, her cropped head bent
tenderly over the dove, her milky eyes
fixed on me with gentle accusation.

In Pissing Alley

My house is cramped, there is no space to sit,
My brain is reeling from some ague or fit
Of words, all borrowed, wrapped in cloth
Of flannel, to preserve the riddling moth.

Not Twickenham, and yet Pope's madmen scrawl
In excrement around my madhouse wall,
Blake's tyger stalks the thickets of my mind,
I sit at Milton's knees, my sockets blind,
And that impatient, marvellous man, John Donne,
Throws me upon my back beneath the sun
To ravish me here on the self-same bed
Where Lucy, Countess Bedford, laid her head.
Beyond my window Marvell's garden lies,
Ten gentle fingers probing at my eyes,
Hopkin's cliffs of fall and Christ the hawk
Are waiting for me on my morning's walk;
Out there, beneath dark trees, the flit and run,
The muslined shade of Emily Dickinson,
And Lucy's in my garden safely dead,
Yet rocks and stones and trees whirl in my head.

There's nothing for it but to take my stick
Where Lowell rages like a lunatic,
And cast about and exorcise the lot.
God's in His Heaven, Pope is in his Grot,
And Willy Yeats' foot upon the floor,
Gives me the signal, "Up, and bar the door."
I clasp my head against a new despair,
A pause, a cough, a step upon the stair,
And passing through the keyhole, wry and thin,
That spectral man, Tom Eliot, enters in.

Well, warm your ghostly shanks around my fire,
No execution equal to desire
Can plague my pen, I abdicate a throne,
And piddle in a gutter of my own.
No need to dig my ribs, of course I know
Great Sappho died three thousand years ago.

In the black mirror shadows pass, repass.
The raging gardener screams, "Keep off the grass".

Zoo Story

Feeding the giraffes in winter sunlight,
they stood like great arched swans
      drinking each other's urine
in an act of love so simple it puts us to shame.

Behind us in the straw-filled manger,
the new-born six-foot child wobbles to life,
its mild eyes luminous. I turn aside,
empty of seed, feeling the tug of life
stir, like a folded flower, put away.

Through the nocturnal house we move together.
The small quiet animals of my childhood stare at me.
Our hands brush by accident, touched by tenderness,
I watch you demonstrate your love for all god's creatures
      but the human ones.
Myself, my son, my grandson, share your zoo,
your pride, your crippled love. They might have been our own;
my gentle son whose love embraces animal, bird, tree, stone,
     & flower, woman & child.

We walk apart,
the bears grumble in their pens,
the white cockatoos parody our babble.
You kiss my forehead.
I watch you walk away,
having shared your ritual ark without a word.

And yet it has remained with me,
the image of us standing there
feeding our carrots to the gentle beasts.

Zoo-Keeper

Stalking your zoo at night,
toucans rip the air, the padding bears & predators,
caged by the swollen water, rock down there
                              under the limestone cliffs.

Your temple & your refuge,
the animals of thought growl in the sunlight,
but at night, a shriek, a claw,
                              twin suffering eyes.

In the nocturnal house,
                    day's night, night's day,
the instincts turn awry
            in that old mockery of the self.

You make your rounds
                  checking the tallies,
                  bolts, bars, cries & exile;
warden of that sad suburban beast
                  that slumbers in the day.

The light flows from the lamp,
the tide laps, fouled with old suicides,
you raise your head, the ape-shaped ribcage
outlined on the sky, & smell yourself,
& turn back into the house.
Your wife stares at a flickering screen,
your dwarf child gambolls there
                              against the light,
                  claiming your arms.
Peacocks flirt coloured tails,
drawing their mocking patterns in the dust,
cicadas buzz like teeth-drills
                  in the palms.
The cage clangs shut.

Hand Holding Violets

You brought me violets once in Martin Place.
We stood on the steps of the granite Post Office
                          giving and receiving
The recorded minute: we played it unrehearsed, unrecognised.

The pincers of the flesh will clasp us tight
And shred our skin like petals.
Violets are death flowers in the Spring rain.

And now I walk, unblessed, in another city,
                          nailed in a narrow room
Lit by sulphurous yellow leaves, the radiator,
                          and the river water.

You lean across the bar, starved small.
The skein of wet-wool stories cocoons against the night,
Feeds your fiery ulcer, warms the single bed
Above the fire-station full of clanging bells.
The landlady, every morning by your inner-spring,
Brings cold toast, God's teeth and hairy diadem
                          wrapped in her kimona.

"Ferrying whisky across to the Islands
For the Yanks; the ack-ack burst like crystal flowers:
Grounded, anxiety neurosis, did my deferred pay
Backing two-year olds: wings clipped in a new suit
Sold insurance to peeling doors on chains.
That bitch I lived with, the sons I've never seen
Since they were knee-high," measured on the bar.

Spells, riddles, games and stories,
The frayed-cuffed hero in the fading light,
The hand, scarred with sun cancers, clutching yellow beer
                          and violets once in Martin Place.

From all redemptive gestures choose this one.

Darby and Joan

> If we'd grown old together
> Our hatreds honed to bone,
> We'd have shared a poisoned afghan robe.
> God bless our hearth and home.

If we'd grown old together,
the arsenic you always thought was in your porridge,
would I have dropped it in?
On either side of the hearth
would we have rocked into oblivion,
savouring the cyanide pellet in the Robur tea,
the hemlock floating in the clear soup from Meals on Wheels?
The unlit gas full on
the loaded gun triggered from the broom cupboard,
straight between your eyes;
the thick blue air
stuffed with "Sunday Suns" under the doors and window sills,
while you took 40 winks.

All those games of hide-and-seek in draughty rooms,
giddy with hate, to fall one day
in the empty hall, and stink like carrion.
Would you have gone on playing clown to my straight man,
bony on the congoleum,
accusing me of kinky infidelities
with old great-uncles building rat's nest cubbies in our yard?
Or perhaps they'd put us side by side in curly
wicker chairs, unravelling on some secluded verandah
in Eventide,
scorpions in a sunny bottle,
to sting ourselves to death,
And then the predestined end;
stone-throwing boys break the glass dome
furred with waxy flowers:
"Beloved wife and husband".

I take our grandchild up,
feeling the generations tug my arms,
trace your features and your liniments
                        through twelve years separation.
Low to high fortune, that's a comedy.
GOD BLESS OUR HEARTH AND HOME.

Look, Look I Have Come Home

I left you, but I always meant
to come back: you forever frozen,
waiting behind the "Herald"
in the bed. I never thought you'd go.
The grass would grow higher, blot out the glass,
the date palm brush the gutters,
the trains rush by to Newcastle & Wynyard.
On the lawn next door a man was always hammering
a glider, it never got off the ground.
One day I'd walk back,
see the shadow of the sunflower on the wall,
its round and furry centre eaten out by bees.
Yesterday I rode past in a train,
saw the home units, all the car yards
strewn with plastic banners.
"Five Ways" the signpost said,
Five Ways to death and madness.
Behind that door my Madame Taussaud's waxworks,
the blue heeler whimpers at your hand.

Homecoming

I

Coming home—the airport filled with strangers,
the case too heavy to carry, the homosexual's kiss.
A deep breath on the gangway, then plunge in,
the panicky claustrophobia, hermetically sealed.
The brutal innocence of noses, pressed to glass,
"Take me, take me."
An empty city, too small to be remembered.

The garden's greened with rain and children's voices,
Outside the sleepout window the maple's rainbow coloured,
brown carnations, from the hospital visit, desolate in vases,
In bed, we touch again, strangers in flesh.

II

A month passes, the maple leaves turn redder,
a fire burns, I read "The New Statesman"
we drink black tea in the garden
you type on the rustic table . . .
we wear clothes to bed.
There is a sense of permanence and comfort.
The Boeing 707 howls across our roof,
My naked body runs across the tarmac
into the dark . . . out of the green garden
and the children coming home from school
                    "Take me . . . Take me."

Anniversary

> Driving back after midnight,
> black streets, empty asphalt, wind.
> Suddenly a rain of yellow leaves.
> They lay in drifts over the wheel hubs,
> clogging the windscreen wipers . . . confetti?
> We were driving home from our wedding,
> an old shoe bumped behind us, full of leaves.

Sparrow Fall

I woke to the fall of a sparrow
and you were gone.
Nothing moved in the dark,
the night went on.

Nobody breathed at my side.
In the open sky
of the window's space, a draught
went out like a sigh.

Stiff in the guttering,
the small sparrow lay.
Its beak gaped, its claws
lifted up to pray.
Cold I lay in the night,
straight I lay in the bed,
only in the first light
I turned my head.

Rocking on two sticks
or down on all fours
to meet hell,
HERE I AM!
Bare-faced,
armoured in bone,
back at that lonely place
where I began.
Anything's possible
now that I am alone,
anything at all,
now Heaven is impossible,
        and all's well.

"While of unsound mind
keep out of the reach of children."
The bottle on the shelf.
The girl sitting dead in the park,
crowned with five robins dropping leaves.
Sitting there . . . all by herself:
they couldn't uncurl her fingers
        from the lysol bottle.
"Don't touch . . . Don't touch."
"Some day MY prince will come."
You old woman in long underpants
crying for Mother.
Feed me *that* poisoned apple . . .

I had forgotten this place:
sitting there, dead in the park,
unconscious of self at last,
robed by robins and swallows, cold.
One does not do it again; the old,
tight-fisted, arthritic, swollen,
lose their grace.

It's a bad joke now; the waiting dark,
so close to us, becomes impossible.
It's so much easier to be braver
                    when it's closer.

Island And Forest

Islands rise out of the sea,
ceremonial, round,
Illyria has two weeping palaces
and a shipwrecked shore.

Crouched under a rock,
your lost child at your side,
eyes dark with dolphins and fishes,
your nets come dripping from the tide.

The island is full of noise,
the boy girdles the earth
with a circling rod of fishes,
but the man stands still in the surf,
the pearls moist in his eyes,
Caliban-Ferdinand-Prospero,
the beast is exorcised,
and the maimed Fisher King by the wreck,
casting his net in the sea,
brings the albatross out by the neck.

Islands are magical rings,
round green circles of fire,
lions roar in the Forest of Arden,
asses bray in the midsummer woods.
We stand deprived in the dark,
to the receding wash of the wave,
Miranda and Ferdinand move
chess pieces in a luminous cave.

Before we break the staff,
and sink into the sea,
here by the southern ocean
I pray for you
on your island.
                    pray for me.

The Gift

Fallen prone in the dark wood,
naked I must face the flood,
in the wood the streaming light
laps me round before the night.
Light irradiates the sky,

from one huge disfigured Eye,
drives me out to stumble blind
through the closets of the mind.
Iron tongue and fire-ball,
clapping bell and raven call,
what dread messages are sent
from the streaming firmament?
The waterworn and shining stone,
sufficient to itself alone,
flashing stream and falling sword,
the round stone that holds the word.
In a green and gentle place
I will hide my marred face,
till the angel in my side
draws her sword and we divide.

I to whiten into bone,
obdurate for death alone,
She to hold the holy stone.

Four Kings

Two kings rose up to meet two kings,
out of a hallowed ground,
and face to face in close embrace
they made no mortal sound,
but silently the kings exchanged
the circle of their crowns.

And two wore flesh, and rosy-limbed
they rode out thigh to thigh,
no armour kept them sacrosanct
under the curved sky;
they met their grisly counterpart
and froze within their eye.

There in the mirror of the lake
I saw them stand like stone,
the one bright hand of flesh embrace
the other hand of bone,
then out across the wintry waste
two kings rode off alone.

The lake runs round in widdershins,
the prophecies in rings,
across the ground in mighty sound
the buzzard's voice sings,
and skeletons in crowns of gold
are substitutes for kings.

Deep in the funnel of the lake,
two smiling youths I found,
they whirled and spun, till one by one,
they sank into the ground;
the deathly kings into the dark
rode on with glittering crowns.

Grave Fairytale

I sat in my tower, the seasons whirled,
the sky changed, the river grew
and dwindled to a pool.
The black Witch, light as an eel,
laddered up my hair
to straddle the window-sill.

She was there when I woke, blocking the light,
or in the night, humming, trying on my clothes.
I grew accustomed to her; she was as much a part of me
as my own self; sometimes I thought, 'She *is* myself!'
a posturing blackness, savage as a cuckoo.

There was no mirror in the tower.

Each time the voice screamed from the thorny garden
I'd rise and pensively undo the coil,
I felt it switch the ground, the earth tugged at it,
once it returned to me knotted with dead warm birds,
once wrapped itself three times around the tower —
                          the tower quaked.
Framed in the window, whirling the countryside
with my great net of hair I'd catch a hawk,
                          a bird, and once a bear.
One night I woke, the horse pawed at the walls,
the cell was full of light, all my stone house
suffused, the voice called from the calm white garden,
                          'Rapunzel'.
I leant across the sill, my plait hissed out
                          and spun like hail;
he climbed, slow as a heartbeat, up the stony side,
we dropped together as he loosed my hair,
his foraging hands tore me from neck to heels:
the witch jumped up my back and beat me to the wall.

Crouched in a corner I perceived it all,
the thighs jack-knifed apart, the dangling sword
                          thrust home,
pinned like a specimen—to scream with joy.

I watched all night the beasts unsatisfied
roll in their sweat, their guttural cries
made the night thick with sound.
Their shadows gambolled, hunch-backed, hairy-arsed,
and as she ran four-pawed across the light,
the female dropped coined blood spots on the floor.

When morning came he put his armour on,
kissing farewell like angels swung on hair.
I heard the metal shoes trample the round earth
                              about my tower.
Three times I lent my hair to the glowing prince,
hand over hand he climbed, my roots ached,
the blood dribbled on the stone sill.
Each time I saw the framed-faced bully boy
                              sick with his triumph.

The third time I hid the shears,
a stab of black ice dripping in my dress.
He rose, his armour glistened in my tears,
the convex scissors snapped,
the glittering coil hissed, and slipped
                              through air to undergrowth.
His mouth, like a round O, gaped at his end,
his finger nails ripped out, he clawed through space.
His horse ran off flank-deep in blown thistles.
Three seasons he stank at the tower's base.
A hawk plucked out his eyes, the ants busied his brain,
the mud-weed filled his mouth, his great sword rotted,
his tattered flesh-flags hung on bushes for the birds.

Bald as a collaborator I sit walled
                              in the thumb-nosed tower,
wound round three times with ropes of autumn leaves.
And the witch . . . sometimes I idly kick
a little heap of rags across the floor.
I notice it grows smaller every year.

RAPUNZEL IN SUBURBIA by Dorothy Hewett

Dorothy Hewett was born in Perth, Western Australia on May 21st, 1923. Nine years a senior tutor in English at the W.A. University she now lives in Sydney, writing poetry and plays on a three year Fellowship from the Australian Council for the Arts. Her poems, short stories and plays have been widely printed and performed in Australia, and a novel, *Bobbin Up,* translated into four foreign languages. Her play, *The Chapel Perilous,* had a season at the Sydney Opera House last year.

Rapunzel in Suburbia is Dorothy Hewett's second collection of poetry. The first was *Windmill Country,* published in 1969. "Dorothy Hewett is a very valuable poet. The poems have an utterance that is calm, intense, candid, individual and often very moving." (Australian Book Review).

"She has the capacity few poets possess of speaking in her own voice with perfect candour and full emotional control, and of writing unselfconsciously about her childhood memories and family myths. This is a valuable book and one whose importance will not be generally appreciated for at least another ten years." (Melbourne Age).

*This first edition is limited to 100 hard bound autographed
copies, and 900 paper bound copies, of which this is number*

Printed by Tonecraft Pty. Ltd., 24B Stanley Street, Peakhurst 2210
and wholly set up by Service Lino Pty. Ltd., Bankstown